Chosen for a
PURPOSE

Compiled by Dr. Mary Segars

ISBN: 978-0-9985511-6-6

TABLE OF CONTENTS

INTRODUCTION

Have you ever found yourself in the midst of a storm, looking up and asking, "Why me?" or in the quiet of a challenging moment, pondering, "Why is this happening to me?" If you have, let me assure you, you're in good company. It's a question as old as time, one that echoes in the hearts of many. But what if I told you that within these questions lies a profound truth, a revelation that you are indeed chosen for a purpose?

In this anthology, "Chosen for a Purpose," we delve into the lives of six remarkable individuals who dared to ask these questions and, in doing so, discovered the powerful truth that there is a purpose for every trial, every challenge, and every seemingly insurmountable obstacle. It may appear as though we're losing, but in reality, we are being positioned for a victory far greater than we could have imagined.

Romans 8:28 (NIV) assures us, "And we know that in all things God works for the good of those who love him, who have been called according to his purpose." This scripture is not just a comforting thought but a foundational truth that underlines the stories you are about to read. Through their unique journey, each author demonstrates that even when the odds seem stacked against us, there is a divine plan at work, shaping, refining, and preparing us for the moment we step into our purpose.

James 1:2-4 (NIV) encourages us, "Consider it pure joy, my brothers and sisters, whenever you face trials of many kinds, because you know that the testing of your faith produces perseverance. Let perseverance finish its work so that you may be mature and complete, not lacking anything." The narratives within these pages are a testament to this process of perseverance, a celebration of the strength that comes from facing and overcoming adversity.

I extend my deepest gratitude to the six courageous authors who have shared their stories and spoken their truths. Their vulnerability and strength are a beacon of hope, illuminating the path for others who may find themselves asking, "Why me?" Through their words, may you discover that you are not merely enduring but are being chosen and prepared for a purpose far greater than you've ever imagined.

Enjoy reading "Chosen for a Purpose." May you find within these pages the strength to persevere, the courage to speak your truth, and the faith to believe that you, too, are chosen for an extraordinary purpose.

Dr. Mary Segars
6 Time Best Seller Author

Dr. Mary Segars

Dr. Mary Segars is the Founder and CEO of Segars Consulting Group. She is committed to providing entrepreneurs and businesswomen the tools needed to be the best leaders in corporate and personal environments. She is a certified John Maxwell Coach, Speaker, and Trainer. Dr. Segars has published two best-selling books; "Power Talk Begins with Power Thought," which is about your "self-talk" to victory, and "Wake Up the Leader Within You," the four steps to awaken the hidden leader within you. She also defines what a leader is and how to lead oneself and others in excellence. She desires to help people tell their stories and speak their truth about their experiences and life. Dr. Segars' Awesome Publishing Company has coached and assisted over 40 authors to become published authors in her four anthologies.

THE BATTLE IS NOT MINE
NATIKA BATTLE

Praise be to the LORD my rock, who trains my hands for war,
my fingers for battle. He is my loving God and my fortress, my
stronghold and my deliverer, my shield, in whom I take refuge,
who subdues peoples under me. Psalms 144:1-2 (NIV)

The literal meaning of battle is to engage in combat between individuals or armed forces.

I came into this world on the battlefield, as I was born not breathing. However, the Lord had other plans for me, and shortly after, I began to breathe on my own. That was only the beginning of knowing that this battle is not mine.

I was the youngest of four girls, the Baby, as my father would call me. With a six-year age difference between my sister right above me, a twelve-year age difference with my second oldest sister, and a fourteen-year age difference with my oldest sister, you can only imagine what life was like for me.

The good thing is I learned a lot of what not to do from my older siblings. The downside is my older siblings were constantly bossing me around. However, my parents would intervene if I was being bossed around too much.

Growing up with such a big age difference and my cousins my age lived miles away, I had to have friends from school to hang out with. I gained three good friends to hang out with who were, as I like to say, mother-approved. My mother was very particular about whom I hung around.

I had a great childhood. I had a friend who had a couple of horses while we were in elementary school. I enjoyed things like going to the YMCA with my friends, sleepovers, and many of the joys of being a child. However, almost drowning at a young age at the YMCA was again the Lord's reminder that it was not my time.

One of the things that my parents, aunts, and uncles made sure of was that I knew the Lord and had a relationship with Him. My mother made sure the friends I was around also knew the Lord. My parents also always prayed for me. I remember peeking into my parent's room many days and watching my father praying on his knees.

Things were good as I began to navigate life from elementary to middle to high school. When I started my first job at McDonalds, I began to have real responsibilities and experience adulthood. This is when I began to see life from a different lens.

I was fortunate to have my cousin Trudy as my manager after a couple of years of working at McDonalds. In that season of my life, I had to put all the things my mother told me about people to use. She would tell me, "It takes all kinds of people to make the world go round." After dealing with some rude, just mean and nasty people while still seeing nice people, I started to understand what that statement meant.

It was in that season when I had to learn to be nice even when people were mean. My mother told me, "You can catch more bees with honey than you can with vinegar," meaning you can win over more people by being polite and kind rather than being mean and unpleasant like them.

While at that job, I purchased my first vehicle with my own money, which I had worked hard for. In this season, I began to have a closer relationship with God since I was able to drive myself to and from church. People saw me working hard, attending school, traveling, and doing things independently. My mother would remind me to put God first even more, watch the company I kept, let the Lord fight for me, and be still and know who God is in my life.

As I began to navigate the workforce, more trials came from car repair to relationships with friends, family, and foes. My cousin Trudy, while working the midnight shift, wrote a prayer for me:

I am the seed of righteousness; my body is strong; my mind is alert. Your word says I can do all things through Christ Jesus, who strengthen me. Your word says no weapon formed against me shall prosper and every tongue that rises against me thou shall condemn. Your word says You bore my grief and carried my sorrow. Lord, I thank you for Your body & blood. You were wounded for my transgression and bruised for my antiques. The chastisement of my peace is upon You, and with Your stripes, I am healed. Father, as I put on the whole armor of God so I can stand against the wilds of the devil, give me wisdom, fresh anointing, and a discerning spirit. Order my steps, and I will give you all the GLORY. AMEN.

I said that prayer every day for over ten years. It wasn't until my late twenties or early thirties that all the talks, prayers, and life situations helped me understand my mother's words, telling me to let the Lord fight my battle and be still. I was even encouraged by the words of Yolanda Adams's song; this battle is not yours; it is the Lord's.

During the season of my life of losing my parents and my grandmother (Big Mama), I felt challenged. If you had a big mama, you know what it is like because she holds the family together. She reminds you of where you come from, your values, cooking, cleaning, morals, and respect for yourself and others. To make things worse, losing your parents is not easy, and the pain seems never to go away. However, there is the blessing of being able to care for them while they are here while always wishing and thinking you could have done more to keep them here. That is the trick the enemy plays with your mind to make you continue feeling the unbearable pain of losing them.

Also, during this season, I gave birth to my daughter. Although doctors told me she would be born with a cleft lip, there was still the battle of the mind. The enemy played with me to make me believe it was my fault. After praying, trusting, and believing in God for everything else to be fine, I had an emergency C-Section due to losing amniotic fluid. My daughter was born prematurely with excited expectations for what happens with premature babies with a cleft lip.

In the next chapter of my life, I dealt with family trials and tribulations, the mishandling of people's feelings, the disrespect, the sense of entitlement, the thinking that one family member is better than the other, and using family members for financial gain, The family physically and mentally fighting, the embarrassment and humiliating one another, cursing out one another, the cheating spouses, lying spouses, the disrespectful children, and the list goes on and on of the things I endured from the people closest to me.

During this time, my mental and physical health was not well. Thoughts of suicide continually ran through my mind. As the divorce was well on its way, my spouse told me, "I cheated because I wanted to many times." I blacked out because I could not believe what my ears had just heard. I ensured that I did things I thought a wife should do. Yet I repeatedly replayed things in my mind, trying to figure out how this happened, why me, and why now. What could I do to prevent this divorce from happening? I was being left with high bills, a child I had to explain all this to, barely enough money to eat, and wondering how I would afford school clothes for the next year. I did not have a mother to call and talk this over with. I had my mother-in-law and only one sister to talk to. They offered great wisdom and knowledge, but pain, hurt, betrayal, and loneliness remained.

After having my child, I began to have some issues in my reproductive system that my doctor could not figure out. After trying several different things and undergoing all types of tests, she found nothing harmful. However, I was having pain to the point it was hurting to walk and, for some periods, kept me in bed for several days. The unexpected menstrual cycle at any given time became an embarrassment. It caused me not to go anywhere or sit or stand for an extended period because I didn't know if my menstrual cycle would come and how heavy it may be. I found a doctor who was the head of OB/GYN at Wayne State University. He immediately scheduled me for an ultrasound and had an ultrasound doctor in the room to diagnose me the same day. I was diagnosed with Adenomyosis, a condition in which endometrial tissue exists within and grows into the uterine wall. It is something that 32% of women deal with. This was something else to add to my list of things to worry about. Now that I knew the issue, I could get the proper treatment.

As I tried to navigate and pray my way through, it seemed as if nothing was working, and things were getting worse by the day. Food was low, money was low, and disconnect notices were coming. I was crying to the Lord for help. But I was embarrassed and afraid to ask for help because I was always the one helping others. God knows my heart, and He sent people from my church family to provide clothes for my daughter. He had a lady from my job bring me frozen food from her home because it was just her and her husband. No one knew what I was going through, but God sent people to help me when I least expected it.

I was still navigating my journey of life. I had not grieved properly over my parents or grandmother. I had not really processed all the mean and hurtful things that family and friends had said and done to me. I was operating with dirt over my pain, and as I moved forward, I was putting dirt over the hurt, which was causing my pain to grow roots in me and stay there, which was indirectly creating triggers, bitterness, and pain.

I had been on my job for over 20 years, and I had a supervisor who intentionally and purposefully found ways to belittle and disrespect me. I tried to do the right thing and have a conversation, only to make things worse. I documented everything and sent it to supervisors, but nothing happened. The harassment got worse, and the more I reported, the worse things got. This, compounded with the years of hurt, pain, and being taken advantage of, felt like nothing was improving. The supervisor made it known that she was a petty supervisor and would do things to harm people's jobs. I decided I was tired and would fight fire with fire.

I began to take things into my own hands with my supervisor and everyone still around. It only took them saying one thing to me, and I read them their rights.

I thank God for praying friends. As I had begun to tell my friend Bam BAM what was happening, she reminded me of Romans 12:19 (NIV), "Do not take vengeance, my dear friends, but leave room for God's wrath, for it is written: it is mine to avenge; I will repay says the Lord."

I understood and began not to allow my supervisor to have power and control over me. It became so hard to go to work every day, not knowing what would happen from day to day. The anxiety, the headache, and the sickness in my stomach were unbearable at times. However, I had someone who depended on me: my daughter. It had gotten to the point I was suspended without pay for five days. Knowing everything I thought I was reporting to her boss was humiliating, yet nothing was being done. My co-workers had begun to see the treatment and knew it was unfair. It became undeniable when I had COVID during the holiday, and even though I had documentation, she told my co-workers I was lying about having COVID. I had to send my COVID results to Human Resources.

It seemed as if it would never end.

Several months after that, someone in our office had COVID, and when you are exposed to someone with COVID, you are to be sent home. The person in the office with COVID turned in my name because she was in contact with me. Even though the protocol was to be sent home, my supervisor and her boss refused to send me home. Human Resources had to get involved for me to be sent home.

This went on for over two years. Proverbs 15:1 (NIV) stood out as I read my Bible: "A gentle answer turns away wrath, but a harsh word stirs up anger."

Although I was reading my word daily and going to church, there were days when I felt defeated and as though I had to defend myself against my supervisor and her supervisor because I was tired of the bullying, harassment, and my co-workers all watching it happen.

Things began to happen as I prayed, fasted, meditated, and called on my prayer warrior friends. As in all my journeys, when I looked at them and realized that when I was calling on the name of Jesus, when I was asking the Lord to pick my friends, when I was singing and praising in my car, house, bathroom, and everywhere else; he heard my cry. As I was reading the book by Joyce Meyers, The Battlefield of the Mind, He was fixing my mind. All the times I sang, this battle is not yours; it is the Lord's; it was an affirmation of my belief.

My mother always told me that as long as you do right by people and they mistreat you, they will always come back. As I sat back and took a trip down memory lane, I realized everything I thought hurt me was for my good. There was purpose in my pain. Those who spoke badly about me - friends, family, or foe - had to come back to me to help me in some shape, form, or fashion. I was promoted away from the supervisor who was harassing me. Her boss, who was allowing the unfair treatment, retired. It was not until I let go and let God fight my battles that I realized that my mother and father had prepared me for the world, but the world was not being prepared for me. As John 15-19-20 states, "If you belonged to the world, it would love you as its own. As it is, you do not belong to the world, but I have chosen you out of the world. That is why the world hates you. Remember what I told you: A servant is not greater than his master. If they persecuted me, they will persecute you also. If they obeyed my teaching, they will obey yours also." It was not until then that I truly understood what it meant to be still and know God. One thing is for sure and for certain: GOD DON'T and did not need my help.

After all the ups and downs, my mother was right: it takes all kinds of people to make the world go round. At the end of the day, we are all God's children, right, wrong, or indifferent.

In the words of Yolanda Adams:

There is no pain Jesus can't feel

No hurt he cannot heal; all things work according to his perfect will; no matter what you're going through, remember God is using you.

There's no sadness Jesus can't feel.

As I look back at the chains that have been broken off of me through breakthroughs and the miracles, signs, and wonders that have taken place in my life, I realize the joy that I have; the world did not give it to me, and the world cannot take it away from me. I thank God for the journey and know that everything I have been through was for my good. God was using me every step of the way. I stayed calling on the name of Jesus through all the storms, even when I did not feel like it. I knew that I could not fight by myself. I knew that the Lord was on the battlefield with me.

I am thankful and grateful for all the Lord has done for me, knowing I am being used by the best.

I needed to be reminded and to remind many of you who have taken time to read this as you navigate this thing called life: No matter what you are going through, God only wants to use you. So, hold your head up high, stick your chest out, and remember this battle is not yours; it is the Lord's.

NATIKA BATTLE

My name is Natika Battle, and I am a contributing author of Amazon's number-one bestseller and multiple other Amazon books. I am a licensed minister and entrepreneur. I studied psychology and health administration at the University of Arizona. I hold certificates in women in leadership and crucial accountability. I have organized impactful conferences such as "Brunch, Browse and Blend" and "I Didn't Know My Own Strength." As a keynote speaker, I have addressed topics such as suicide prevention at local community events and "Dive into Faith" in Grand Prairie, Texas. My unwavering faith in God has guided me through life's challenges, including caregiving and personal struggles. I have faced and overcome mental, physical, emotional, and spiritual trials and can attest to the transformative power of faith. I am a living testimony to the belief that our battles are not ours alone but entrusted to the Lord.

My Determination, My Lifeline
Fredricka Leenice DuPree

"Run hard and fast in the faith. Seize the eternal life, the life you were called to, the life you so fervently embraced in the presence of so many witnesses." I Timothy 6:12 (MSG)

This verse encourages us to remain steadfast and committed in our faith journey, embracing the eternal life that comes through faith in Christ Jesus. It is a call to perseverance and dedication when faced with challenges. In hindsight, this verse should have been an anthem or daily affirmation, perhaps my mantra. Only God knew the days that would come.

Jesus Christ himself was put through numerous tests, trials, and tribulations. He has shown us how to come out victoriously without reacting. Remaining prayerful, meek, humble, and silent will allow us to pass tests.

Caterpillars go through a metamorphosis to become butterflies. They go from a low place of crawling on their bellies to a high place of beauty and flight.

The low place began early in childhood after our family was disjointed due to my father's infidelity. It was a downward spiral to my virtual hell after that. My primary caregiver, being overcome with devastation about losing her family as she had once known it to be for the past 12 years, was rough. Therefore, I became the person for whom all the frustration was released through the worst emotional, physical, and verbal abuse and neglect imaginable. This did wonders for my self-esteem. NOT! I never felt safe or protected after Daddy left unless he was present. This was a lonely and miserable time.

I became a teen mother at the age of 16. What a disappointment to the family, church, and community in the 1980's. At that time, you are dragged alone to the front of the church to apologize for your sin, even though you didn't commit it alone. You were also removed from regular school to attend a school for pregnant girls until after the delivery of the baby. Then, you were kicked out of the family home due to embarrassment. WHEW! What a grand start at such an early age. Now what? Where do I go without resources or support? My favorite aunt, God rest her soul, opened her doors to us without issue. This was not the best environment to raise a child because it was a non-stop party and revolving door of people. It was the opposite of my upbringing, but I was grateful to have a place to stay. The never-ending party was initially intriguing to someone who had never seen this part of life but would soon grow old for someone who yearned for more. I quickly sought other housing because this was no way to live and raise a child.

One of my siblings' families was not too far away, literally down the street, and they allowed us to move in. At least this environment was more like home - safe, clean, and spirit-filled. I was able to re-enter school and seek employment.

There would be years of tumultuous relationships while having little contact with my primary caregivers for at least a decade. Finally, I entered my first stable romantic relationship that lasted until my child was four years old. I left because he did not want me to be independent of him – no work, no school. I couldn't even grocery shop alone. I have no objections to being a kept woman, but that was EXTREME.

After that, I met and married my prince charming, who would take me from all the trouble and instability and spend a large part of my life with him. He was great to my two children. This would be the happiest I had been since before Daddy left home. He was my safe place, my everything; we were each other's "Kiss of Life." We blended families well. Our marriage started something in his family. Soon, his family members, who had been cohabitating for years, began to marry. They were very family-oriented. This was home. We worked cohesively as a team and had fun daily just being in each other's presence. He cared for the home, me, and the children as he should have. This was the heaven any woman dreams of until it wasn't. Little did I know he would also be the one who would shatter me even more than I had already been. This part of my life would break, bruise, and almost wipe me out.

My wonderful husband came home from work one day and informed me he smoked a 51 (marijuana joint laced with cocaine) and liked it. I was so naïve I said, "Well, okay honey, just don't do it again." After he disclosed the use, in hindsight, I know now that was not his first time. He was more than likely reaching a point of being out of control and seeking help. I was so far removed from the world and the things of the world that I could not see it. The addiction (at that time, I didn't know this was what he was going through or what it was called) had gotten worse. The blessing in this situation is he maintained employment and continued doing everything as usual. It was not the scenario we typically envision with drug addicts, where the person sells everything in the house, including the kitchen sink. My hubby continued spending time with our children; he entertained, attended church services, and was so good to us. I didn't notice anything, but I guess I wouldn't because I didn't know what to look for other than the extremes. I guess he was good at covering his tracks. Apparently, as the drug use increased, his appearance and moods began to change.

Eventually, hubby entered Harbor Light, an in-patient rehabilitation center in downtown Detroit. The third rehabilitation center, Shar House on the west side of Detroit, would be his saving grace. Our marriage did not survive due to infidelity after he became clean. I left feeling bruised, worn, bitter, thrown away, and never thought I would love again. I felt this beautiful man I loved so much and held everything down for while he was getting himself together would move on and give all that goodness to some undeserving person while I put in all the work. Now, me and the children would be left all alone to navigate this cruel, cold world again.

After the divorce, I maintained any job position that worked around my children's schedule while I attended college. There was no job beneath me. If it paid a decent wage, I would work as long as the schedule did not interfere with my children's schedule. The employers knew my children and home came first. The temporary agency was my best friend. I could work and get paid a decent wage without commitment. I wanted my children to see and feel my presence. I wanted them to know I was always nearby. I definitely want them to know, without a shadow of a doubt, that they are LOVED. I still have a question in my mind: "Do my parents love me"? It did not matter what had to be done; it was done. Carpooling every morning, cooking and having dinner as a family, playtime, sleepovers, completing homework assignments, attending all parent-teacher conferences, dance classes, martial arts, music lessons, DAPCEP on Saturday, and summer programs were the highlights of my life.

I would take the children to school with me and set them up for a couple of hours while I was in class; we were a team. I used every situation to make it appear an adventure for them. They never knew we were having difficulties. I did not know, at that time, that I was applying spiritual principles.

Through this process, I began to realize how the Lord covered us in EVERYTHING. He covered us emotionally, financially, mentally, and spiritually. The Word says in Psalm 27:10 (NCV), "If my father and mother leave me, the Lord will take me in."

I was left in situations that seemed impossible, but I never lost my mind. I was in places with severe substance use and abuse and did not give in to use of them at that time. Church attendance ceased, but the God in me never left. We were given favor despite the rising cost of housing. The cost for us remained far below market rate until I could purchase my own home. Even during the housing crash of 2008, when we lost our home and I was simultaneously laid off from work, we were immediately blessed with another home by my colleague and good friend Sharon and her husband, Connie. God always had His hand on me, my children, and my situation. I must be honest and transparent with you: I did not look at any of these as blessings at that time. For example, the new home was almost 100 miles away and secluded from everyone and everything familiar. Rather than seeing it as a blessing to have a new home, I was distracted by the distance.

God does His best handiwork in the dark and in seclusion. Beautiful babies grow in darkness. Pearls, once the most highly regarded jewel only worn by European nobility, are created in darkness far below the sea's surface by hurt, injury, and pain. Diamonds, the girl's best friend, are created in the darkest, deepest pits of mines under the most stringent pressure and the hottest heat. Once the diamonds and pearls have come forth, they have become something rare, fine, admirable, and valuable: Kingdom of God's "Pearl of Great Price." Just as diamonds and pearls have become something of value, even more valuable have I become with all of my perfect imperfections.

Life has its way of lifing as we say these days. My pastor always says during his sermons, "If you don't get a handle on the issue, the issue will get a handle on you." I never had the opportunity to grieve any of the losses or any of the situations that occurred during my life at all whatsoever. That was so AMAZING to me. I suffer in silence probably because I grew up in the era of "what goes on in this house, stays in this house." I Learned to smile when there should be tears. Those closest to me over the years would always inquire how I dealt with everything. I always had the same response, "I just keep it moving; I don't have time to think about it." Well, that is so very true. Life continued to move. I never discussed the issues, so I moved as if nothing ever happened.

Furthermore, I wanted my children to experience a normal, healthy childhood. I wanted them to be children for as long as possible. My childhood didn't last too long at all. It was over around ten years old and definitely moved into adulthood at 16. My objective and goal were to shield my beautiful children from as much hurt, harm, and danger as a mother possibly could. I wanted to protect, teach, and give them as much LOVE and wonderful memories as a person can humanly stand.

Fast forward to 2020, the year of COVID-19. I had suffered from migraine headaches since I was a teen. Doctors had given numerous tests and never found a root cause for them. A specialist prescribed migraine medication that never worked. During this same time of uncertainty, I thought I found solace at the bottom of a wine bottle to rid myself of the pain. Needless to say, that did not work. I was home alone, and the world was at a standstill as we were forced to shelter in place. I had no alternative but to look at myself and listen to my inner self and thoughts day in and day out. Everything that I had gone through from early childhood until adulthood came back to my remembrance; even those things I had tucked into the sea of forgetfulness to remember them no more returned, and I was forced to finally deal with every situation, every feeling, every emotion. GEESH! This was a very traumatic experience but good at the same time. The day of reckoning had come. My true healing and deliverance were finally here, but this would not happen in a single day. This was an ordeal, to say the least.

After my "yes," I was healed, delivered, and set free. God has given us the ministry of reconciliation. Abandoned, cheated on, dejected, rejected, unwanted, and told I would never be anything, be anyone, do anything, or be loved by anyone; if you apply the ministry of reconciliation, this will provide healing and give you hope for everything you've been through in your life. Look at God! He uses EVERYTHING in our lives to His Glory.

There is always a light at the end of the tunnel. As a mother, I learned a lot about myself while rearing my own children, thus understanding my children and parents more. We can only use the tools we have to do the job. When we learn better, we do better. So, sharpen the tools as you learn to do better, and then pay it forward. Philippians 1:6 (MSG), "Being confident of this, that he who began a good work in you will carry it on to completion until the day of Christ Jesus." It is a reminder that there will always be issues, problems, setbacks, and circumstances en route to the promise.

Life does not have to end due to challenges. We must not allow the challenges to make us bitter but better. It is easier said than done when left to your own devices. Nevertheless, this may all be done with the help of our Lord and Savior, Jesus Christ. Our brokenness is for a purpose, not just for the sake of being broken. I began low, broken, angry, afraid, bitter, hurt, and pregnant as a teen. Now I am pregnant with vision, dreams, inspiration, joy, and better than ever and have given birth to businesses, my babies: Nurse Nikki who manages a rehab facility in the greater Detroit area and owns Angelic Companions home care and adult foster care, Ray is an aviation manager at FedEx Air and CEO of Life Events Insurance Hub in Memphis, Tennessee, and Vee is a full-time nursing student, full-time CENA, aspiring pediatrician, and owner/operator of Adorned Beauty Make-Up (artist and products) currently in the greater Detroit area.

I am so proud to say my first stable is doing great, and ex-hubby has been clean and sober for 31 years and now co-pastors a beautiful edifice with his wife. We have great relationships with our children and grandchildren – "it takes a village."

My relationship with both sets of parents and all siblings is PHENOMENAL, and I am Migraine and alcohol-FREE! We serve a mighty and awesome God.

We may not pass all the tests the first time, but eventually, after failing forward multiple times, we will WIN! Exercising our faith and spiritual muscles will yield great results.

I was Determined to live life on its own terms and keep my head when everyone else was losing theirs.

I was Determined to create stability for my children in the midst of great instability.

I was Determined to overcome obstacles and defy the odds in the face of adversity.

I was Determined to reach my goals and help others attain theirs in the process.

I was Determined to use every gift to the Glory of God and return to Him an increase.

I was Determined to wait on the Lord and be of good cheer and not be tired by waiting.

I am Determined that I am a WINNER, and I declare and decree that I am WINNING, and this is indeed MY WINNING SEASON!

FREDRICKA LEENICE DUPREE

Fredricka Leenice DuPree is the first of 8 children from Detroit, Michigan, a Minister and Proclaimer of The Gospel of Jesus Christ. She earned a Master's in Business Administration with a concentration in Strategic Management from Davenport University. She has a Bachelor of Science in Criminal Justice from the University of Detroit Mercy – all with honors. She is an Advanced Certified Paralegal and CEO of Specialized Legal Docs. She serves as Executive Administrator of Life Events Insurance Hub based in Memphis, Tennessee, and is a licensed insurance broker in several states. She serves as a Case Management Consultant for Evans Counseling Solutions to coach and mentor at-risk women and youth. She is also a caregiver and advocate for her four parents and others. The family has affectionately named her "Mama Niecy" for the way she steps in to ensure everyone is cared for appropriately and receives ALL available resources. She is known for her tenacity, perseverance, fighting for the underdog, and WINNING.

That's why we know, Fredricka Leenice DuPree, this is your WINNING SEASON!!

FROM PLANS TO PURPOSE – MY 'AHA' MOMENT
BARBRA GENTRY-PUGH

There are moments in life when our plans, no matter how meticulously crafted, are suddenly interrupted by a divine whisper that redirects our path. For me, this came in the form of an 'Aha' moment ~ a Kairos Moment! It was a moment that if I am truly honest, I was not ready to hear. However, a clear and unmistakable message from God stopped me in my tracks, informing me that it was not yet time to launch the ministry I had envisioned around 'The Kairos Life Plan,' which I had developed and worked on for over a year. I fully embraced the concept and felt that this was where God was leading me to share with His women.

The Kairos concept and Kairos Moments impassioned me. I changed the name of my website and logo to Kairosbenterprises to reflect the conception of the ministry I had anticipated. I also developed a Facebook group entitled "Kairos Moments for Women of Faith" to undergird my message shared in the 'The Kairos Life Plan.' My heart was set on launching the program, and I had invested countless hours into crafting a program and launching a ministry that I believed would transform lives. The idea was rooted in a deep desire to provide women with a collaborative and strategic process for an exploratory pathway that moves them towards personal healing and restoration from the wounds of life to live holistic and impactful lives through transformational relationships. However, little did I know God had a different timeline in mind.

For years, the concept of "Kairos" has fascinated me. It started as a seed planted in my heart in 2004 while completing my thesis for a Master's Degree in Christian Education from Michigan Theological Seminary, now Moody Theological Seminary-Michigan. Although the seed was not fully mature, it continued to germinate. After graduation, I put it on the mental shelf of my heart and mind, and over the years, I would reflect on it in my writings and ministry. I felt in my heart that one day, I would have the opportunity to develop a program and launch a ministry.

WHAT IS KAIROS?

What Kairos is, and how does it relate to the life God has designed for us? The Greeks have two words for time. Chronos (χρόνος) is quantitative and refers to chronological or sequential (clock) time, and Kairos (καιρός) is a time of a qualitative, permanent nature, and refers to God's time! Kairos signifies a proper or opportune time for action. Being qualitative, it is timeless, meaning the right, critical, proper time, or season. It is an opportune time, a call for action, conversion, and transformation. However, by definition, kairos means more than 'mere time or season.' It's like a perfect moment, a special opportune moment in time when God acts.

KAIROS MOMENTS!

A kairos moment occurs when it is God's time to act in our lives. It is a decisive moment in time when God gives us the opportunity to respond. It is a precise moment when God creates an opportunity for essential growth and incredible transformation. God often works behind the scenes of our lives. When this happens, He will interrupt the pace of our day to get our attention for what He has for us. This is a defining moment, a Kairos Moment, a favorable moment within time when God acts, and we respond. It is a specific moment that God has designed for us to respond to what He has for us. When we respond, it positions us for a life-changing and transformative moment for us to walk in our purpose and reach our destiny!

After God gave me a renewed and persevering heart, in September 2020, Kairos-B-Enterprises, LLC was formed. As Founder and CEO, I felt ready to step into my divine assignment. I felt my message was increasingly clear, and I was ready to step into my divine purpose. I was ready to fully introduce my program and assist Christian women in living Kairotically - a life shaped by God's will to walk in wisdom and purpose. This would position women of faith to recognize and respond to their Kairos Moments, NEVER to miss God's best for their lives, and to live more intentionally.

One of my favorite authors is Robert Mulholland Jr., author of "Shaped by the Word," one of my references for my thesis. He emphasized a new way to read Scripture. A way that allows Scripture to shape your spiritual life. It helps you to learn to listen to the voice of God in the Word of God. To move from informational reading to formational reading of the God's Word. He emphasized giving up control over the text and letting God lead your reading and understanding. This concept literally changed my life. It was in his book. "Shaped by the Word, The Power of Scripture and Spiritual Formation" shaped my whole biblical frame of reference by meditating on the Word of God. This formational approach to reading God's Word can bring you to a more vibrant relationship with God. Only through formational reading of the Bible will you find yourself shaped by the Word of God. In this book, I was also introduced to the concept of "Kairos" and the "Kairotic Existence" in chapter seven. In the first paragraph, he invites the reader to be still in God's presence. He goes on to say for the reader to take a few moments as we begin this chapter to recollect ourselves in the presence of God and open our hearts, our minds, and our beings to whatever God wants to do with us. This was followed by a prayer:

Oh God, once again we turn to You. We come to You in our incompleteness, that you might complete us. We come to You in our brokenness that you might make us whole. We come to you in our "dis-ease" that you might heal us. Help us to open the deeps of our lives to You, that in this chapter, and in all of this book, You will be able to work in us that which you purpose for us, in your perfect will for our wholeness. Stir our heart, stimulate our minds, and have your way with us. For all You are doing, for all You are going to do, we give you praise and thanks in Jesus' name, Amen.

I fell in love with the entire book as the author outlined scripturally and biblically the concept of Kairos and the Kairotic Existence. He outlined Kairos Moments and the importance of these concepts in the lives of us as Believers in Christ. I fully embraced the Kairos concept and how Kairos Moments played a crucial role in our lives. They are life-changing and transformative moments God places in our lives that change our perspectives and life trajectories.

Later in May 2021, while participating in an anthology project, "Gathering The Fragments That Nothing Would Be Lost'" I felt the hand of God preparing me for the next level of the Kairos concept. Upon completing the anthology and working with my coach then, I felt that it became increasingly clear what God was doing. The seed was ready to spring forth, and I was ready to move forward.

"There are moments in history when a door for massive change opens.
Great revolutions, either good or evil, spring up in the vacuum
created by these openings. In such divine moments, key
men, women, and entire generations risk everything
to become the hinge of history, the 'pivot point'
that determines which way the
door will swing."
~Lou Engle

Throughout my years of working in women's ministry, I had the privilege of walking alongside women from all walks of life, helping them navigate their spiritual journeys, and supporting them as they sought to understand their identity in Christ. I believed I was walking and serving in my purpose, fulfilling my calling by fostering environments where women could grow, heal, and flourish. I attempted to create an atmosphere for women of all ages who faced real-life challenges to be provided with real-life solutions and the opportunity to live holistic and balanced lives through transformational relationships with the heartbeat of God so that they could be better women, wives, mothers, and citizens of the kingdom.

I longed to see women living out their faith more effectively, as life is real! I knew and talked to women who came to church hurting and went home hurting! Listening to their struggles and issues made me feel compelled to do more. I sought to provide opportunities for women to come to know God's love as they learned more about living unpretentious and godly lives.

I believe the heartbeat of women's ministry is empowering women to share, grow, and mature in all areas of their lives physically, emotionally, socially, financially, and spiritually; to follow God intimately, serve Him authentically, and share Him confidently with others who do not know Him as their Lord and Savior, Jesus Christ.

MY LIFE'S SCRIPTURE!

"But my life is worth nothing to me unless I use it for finishing
the work assigned me by the Lord Jesus the work of telling
others the Good News about the wonderful grace of God."

Acts 20:24 (NLT)

There are times in life when we have asked ourselves, God, why am I here? What is my divine assignment? Am I walking in my calling, God's divine purpose, and others? Mark Twain stated, "The two most important days in your life are the day you are born, and the day you find out why." One thing is for sure: you are not here by accident, and every life matters to God! Scripture is very clear as to what our purpose in life should be. Solomon, one of the wisest men who ever lived, discovered the futility of life when it is lived only for this world. Solomon says in Ecclesiastes 12:13-14 "Here is the conclusion of the matter: Fear God and keep His commandments, for this is the whole duty of man. For God will bring every deed into judgment, including every hidden thing, whether it is good or evil." He is saying that life is all about honoring God with our thoughts and lives, thus keeping His commandments, and that we will one day stand before Him in judgment. So, part of our purpose in life is to fear God and obey Him.

Sadly, many are wasting precious time being self-absorbed, angry, spiteful, focusing only on material possessions and power/control, living in the past, blaming others and/or life's circumstances for where they are in life, wondering who loves or does not love them or giving too much value on what others think. Jesus said if you belong to me, STOP! You can make your divine assignment godly easy or hard. God will do exactly what He says in Philippians 1:6, "Being confident of this, that he who began a good work in you will carry it on to completion until the day of Christ Jesus."

What does God have to do to get our attention so that we can fulfill His assignment? Several years while attending a USANA Regional Conference in Orlando, Florida, I had the privilege and honor to personally meet one of the speakers, Nick Vujicic, an Australian Evangelist. If you are unfamiliar with him, he was born with no arms or legs. I was amazed at how powerful he was as he spoke. Listening to him was not only convicting but also a humbling experience. Part of his testimony was how he prayed to God to give him arms and legs. God did not answer his prayer, and later, he tried to drown himself in the bathtub. He later gave his life to Christ at the age of 15. Today, he is in his forties, graduated from a university, started his own business, has a wife and son, and shares the message of HOPE and the gospel of Jesus Christ to millions, and yes, with no arms or legs.

My passion is to see women being fulfilled in what they believe their calling and purpose to be. This caused me to struggle in my heart and my relationship with some in authority in the church. It appeared that some women were not sure or knowledgeable about their role as women of God, and often, the things God required of them was secondary. Even more challenging to grasp was that some other women did not seem to recognize that living out their faith involved doing more than attending church services. There were often no ministries to biblically address how to live holistically balanced lives, addressing their emotional and spiritual lives and how it often affected their physical lives. This challenged me greatly in this season of my life, causing me to walk more closely with the Lord than I ever had before. Consequently, my faith became stronger, and I was more solid in the courage of my convictions. I was also better able to allow others to be who they choose to be until they were convicted and ready to see life differently, allowing me to trust God to love them through their difficulties as He has done with me.

INTRODUCTION: FROM PLANS TO PURPOSE ~ MY 'AHA' MOMENT

I had always believed I was walking in my purpose. For years, my passion was to guide women towards living a holistic life, helping them seize those divine moments to step into their God-given destiny. I was involved in various aspects of outreach and community ministry. As previously noted, my previous life's work has allowed me to develop the Kairos Life Plan, an Evidence-Based Biblical Plan for healing the physical, emotional, and spiritual impediments that hinder the metamorphic processes of life. I was committed to providing a collaborative and strategic process for an exploratory pathway that moves women towards personal healing and restoration from the wounds of life to live holistic, balanced, and impactful lives. My experience in the areas of critical and behavioral health medicine, completing thousands of assessments and counseling, has set the stage for a greater understanding of human behavior and the interrelatedness of mind, body, and spirit to be equipped to walk in freedom and live a transformed life - a Kairotic Life.

I believed my focus was clear, my mission well-defined, and my heart fully committed. This dedication was particularly evident in my work within the church and outreach women's ministry. I spent countless hours encouraging and empowering women to discover and live out their purpose. But then, in a moment of profound clarity, everything shifted – an 'Aha' Moment.

An 'Aha' moment, often referred to as a moment of sudden insight or realization, is a powerful experience that can lead to significant changes in one's life direction. This moment can occur during a time of reflection, after receiving advice, or as a result of a culmination of experiences. It's a moment where everything seems to click, and your path becomes clearer. Psychologically, an 'Aha' moment is linked to the brain's ability to make connections between disparate pieces of information, leading to a new understanding. It's often associated with a feeling of relief, clarity, and motivation to take action.

It was an ordinary day, much like any other. I was engrossed in my work, crafting programs and strategies centered around the "Kairos Life Plan," when a sudden realization struck me, one so powerful it felt as if the very ground beneath me had shifted. It was an 'Aha' moment, a moment when God peeled back the layers and revealed a more profound truth that had been quietly stirring within me all along: my purpose wasn't just about helping others live in the moment and responding to God for a moment of divine transformation; it was something much deeper, it was about healing, a deeper healing, it was Healing From Within!

In that instant, I saw it clearly! I experienced my "Aha / Kairos Moment! God was teaching me all alone to experience what I had been sharing with others. He allowed me to experience a shift so powerful that it got my attention in such a powerful way that I could not mistake it or deny that it was straight from the mind of God. I am so grateful for my Kairos Moment!

The women I am called to serve don't just need guidance on navigating life's pivotal moments; they need healing from the past hurts and emotional wounds that were silently sabotaging their present and future. They needed to be set free from the chains of unresolved pain, bitterness, and shame, issues of the heart that were manifesting as physical ailments, emotional distress, and spiritual stagnation, and to guide others through the often painful but ultimately redemptive process of inner healing.

This revelation was both liberating and unmanning. It meant I had to pivot, to move away from a focus that had defined my work for several years, and step into a new focus. Yet what was interesting was that God had already prepared me for this work. Through my training and work in medical/surgical and psychiatric nursing, outreach ministry/mentoring, and biblical counseling, I gained insights into the root causes of various diseases, conditions, and syndromes that can afflict and harm us, perpetuating our illnesses.

My career/work and involvement in coordinating psychiatric services enabled me to observe potential triggers of physical and emotional disorders, often intertwined with the spiritual condition, specifically addressing 'the issues of the heart,' such as anger, bitterness, resentment, guilt, shame, and others. The body, mind, and spirit function harmoniously to shape your identity. Who you are and everything you do emanates from the condition of your heart. Your heart's emotional and spiritual condition significantly influences all aspects of your life, as what you experience emotionally/spiritually can manifest how you feel physically! Doing thousands of physical and behavioral assessments has prepared me to dig deeper to confront not just symptoms but root causes that require healing from within.

WHY PURPOSE?

Practically speaking, purpose provides direction, motivation, and fulfillment. It was in the mind of the Creator before we were born. Without a clear sense of purpose, we can easily become lost, drifting from one thing to another without ever truly finding satisfaction. Purpose drives us to get up each morning with a sense of anticipation and commitment. It keeps us moving forward, even when the road is difficult or unclear. God designed it to solve a problem in the earth's realm. When we do not discover what that problem is, we become the problem.

The Bible teaches us that purpose is not merely about what we do but about who we are called to be in Christ. Proverbs 19:21 reminds us, "Many are the plans in a person's heart, but it is the Lord's purpose that prevails." This verse has always resonated with me, but in that 'Aha' Moment, its truth became more evident than ever. My plans, though well-intentioned, were just that, my plans. But God had a greater purpose, one that would lead not only to transformation in my life but also to the healing of others.

My 'Aha' Moment was a clarion call to realign my life with God's purpose. It was a shift from focusing on external achievements to addressing the internal, often hidden, wounds that hold us back. Understanding that my true purpose was to help others find healing from within didn't just change my work's trajectory; it transformed how I viewed the Christian life. It brought a new depth to my faith and a greater clarity to my calling.

The biblical concept of purpose goes beyond personal ambition; it's about aligning our lives with God's will. Romans 8:28 assures us, "And we know that in all things God works for the good of those who love him, who have been called according to his purpose." This is the foundation upon which our lives must be built, not just pursuing goals but embracing the divine calling that God has placed on our lives, one that often leads us to unexpected and profound places. My story is a shift of how God took my plans and turned them into a purpose far greater than I had imagined. It's a journey from focusing on moments to understanding the importance of healing the heart, mind, and spirit. It's about embracing the truth that real freedom and true purpose begin when we are healing from within.

This divine pause was not a denial but a redirection, urging me to focus instead on the wealth of experiences and insights I had gained through years of working in medicine and counseling. Through these experiences, I witnessed firsthand the profound connection between the mind, body, and spirit. I came to understand that unresolved emotional and spiritual issues could manifest in physical ailments and that true healing requires addressing the whole person. This realization was the catalyst that propelled me toward my true purpose—a purpose not anchored in my original plans but in God's perfect timing and design for my life.

Looking back, I see how God was preparing me for this new direction all along. My years in women's ministry were not just about helping others but also about shaping me and refining my understanding of what true purpose looks like. As I counsel women through their struggles, I began to notice a pattern: many of the issues faced, whether physical, emotional, or spiritual, were deeply rooted in unresolved pain and brokenness. This insight became the cornerstone of my new understanding of purpose.

God singles us out to serve, but training is required to get us to wholeness. The wholeness comes when everything is counted, weighed, measured, and considered, and nothing is omitted. Preparing us for HIS

Service may include a journey through an "Aha" Moment and a Kairos Moment!

I am reminded of 2 Corinthians 4:7. "But we have this treasure in jars of clay, to show that the surpassing power belongs to God and not to us." (ESV) I have this treasure, this gift inside of me deposited by God with an assignment ahead of me and anointed by God to reach my destination for the glory of God. God singles us out to serve, but training is required to get us to wholeness. The gift is transferred from one to another. The wholeness comes when everything is counted, weighed, measured, and considered, and nothing is omitted. Preparing us for HIS Service may include a journey through an "Aha" Moment to healing from within!

Barbra Gentry-Pugh

Barbra is CEO & Executive Director of Kairos-B-Enterprises, LLC., Heart Expressions Ministries International, a faith-based ministry devoted to reaching the heart of women one beat at a time, to live lives expressing the heartbeat of God.

Barbra is a Transformational Speaker, Certified International Life Coach, and Certified Biblical Counselor.

Barbra is an internationally published Award-Winning Author. Barbra is a PWN International Literary Award Recipient for her first book, "Every Beat of My Heart," and her debut book release.

Barbra has over 30 years of working in ministry as President of Women's Ministries and Outreach Ministries. Barbra's passion is to see women healed from the wounds of life, live holistic and balanced lives, and walk in freedom and purpose. Her life Scripture is Acts 20:24, "But my life is worth nothing to me unless I use it for finishing the work assigned me by the Lord Jesus, the work of telling others the Good News about the wonderful grace of God."

Website: https://barbragentrypugh.com

WATCH ME NOW
RUTH E. KING

It's been ten years since the death of my husband. Ruth had to change her entire life. But God always has a plan, as stated in Jeremiah 29:11(AMP):

> For I know the plans and thoughts that I have for you,' says the
> Lord, 'plans for peace and well-being and not for disaster, to
> give you a future and a hope.

Ruth is a control freak. I don't like surprises. I need to know what's happening. Everything that I previously did with my husband, now I have to do alone. It's okay! I had never lived alone and had to overcome my fear.

> For God has not given us a spirit of fear, but of power and of
> love and of a sound mind. (II Timothy 1:7)

Let me give you a few examples... I now have to take my own garbage to the curb. I have to pump my own gas. Here's the tricky one: get into a dress that needs to be zipped. Don't laugh. I cried. But I figured out a way to do this. Put my jewelry on. No more crying, Ruth King. The enemy wanted me to lose sight of ministry and dwell on what I could not do. Watch me!

Since my husband's death, I had to realize that "ministry" is still in me even though ministry at that time was with my husband. I get it!

I always knew I was called to be a Praise & Worship Leader, Intercessor, Teacher, and Preacher. I have been through so much as a woman I knew my ministry was for women. So, the Lord and I have had many conversations.

I have been singing since the age of four. Back in the day, we didn't have Praise & Worship. We had Testimony Service. I was trained for that at the age of 14. Testimony Service was when the saints either testified or sang a song. If no one got up, as the leader, you carried on with the songs.

As a spirit-led Praise & Worship Leader, you and God become one. You cannot take the people where you have never been. As the Leader, you need to take the people into the Presence of God. As the Leader, you have to hear the Voice of the Lord. Oh, how I heard His Voice so clearly. He would bring songs to my remembrance and even give me songs straight from HIM.

Even when I was under attack by the enemy, I would still show up to do my job as Worship Leader. I was like the woman in the Bible with the issue of blood. The blood flowed non-stop. It was very uneasy. But when you have had an encounter with God, you continue to do what you have been called to do. Watch me!

The next thing I was called to do was to lead the women's ministry. This was my heart. We did so much together. However, my favorite thing was to go to the women's shelters and minister to them, even those with children. We knew they felt unloved and not cared for. So we went in periodically, did hair and nails, and brought toiletries and clothing for them. But most importantly, we shared the Word of God, which is John 3:16 (KJV):

> For God so loved the world, that he gave his only begotten Son,
> that whosoever believeth in him should not perish, but have
> everlasting life.

After that, I developed a Bereavement Ministry. This was birthed out of my needing someone to assist me when my Mother passed. I was clueless. The only thing I knew was the number to the funeral home because it was constantly repeated on the radio. People under pressure to make arrangements should have someone not part of the family accompany them. When you are upset, you make irrational decisions. Believe it or not, this is how funeral homes make their money. So, I left a manual I created to assist people in their time of need. Ministry, right? Watch me!

So, I left that church of over ten years and came to another church. Unable to do Praise & Worship there because he wanted professional singers, it bothered me. But I knew I was sent there to do ministry. Before I joined the church, the Pastor asked me to lead the team that takes in people who want salvation and want to join. This was good. But it wasn't the reason I was sent there.

I was then asked to assist with the Bible School. In doing that, I also began to teach classes on what I knew best: Prayer and Intercession. Ministry... Watch me!

My mother was my greatest example of an intercessor. I remember hearing my mother calling on God In the wee hours of the night. We called her home "Prayer Headquarters."

I knew there was more for me. I went on to preside over our services. To be a Presider, you had to do prayer and scripture to open up; if the Pastor didn't show up, you had to preach. I knew this was part of my calling. During this time, again, the enemy was mad at me. Some Sundays, I couldn't even talk due to sinus infections. But I was there in place if no one else was. Watch me!

Then "COVID" happened. Everything changed. No one was doing anything. The world is on lockdown.

COVID is over. The world has been released. Where do I go from here, right? I was not asked back to my previous position and felt empty and useless. I was asking God, "Where are you? I know you are not through with me yet!"

I received a call from a friend who lived here in Michigan and moved to New Orleans (a place I had never been before). She said she was having a women's conference and wanted little ole me to be one of the speakers. I said yes!

Why? I had never spoken at a women's conference before. I started to call her back because it made me so nervous. This would mean I had to fly out alone and stay in the hotel alone. Remember, I don't like being alone. But the Holy Spirit said to go! I am so glad I did. I spoke on Friday night as well as Saturday afternoon. I had my notes, but God had other plans. I met so many wonderful women. I was truly encouraged. But you know, in the midst of God's blessing, the enemy has to show up. We had a hard time getting back home and were delayed a day. But I had a great time! Watch me!

After that, I was asked to speak at a church anniversary. I had never done that either. My Pastor-Friend called me while I was in my car. She said the Lord told her to call me. Again, little ole me? She stated she had other speakers. But she wanted me to be the main speaker. Lord, please help me. God blessed in this! Watch me!

Meanwhile, on this journey, I have been a part of two groups. One is a group of prophets. I did tell them I am NOT a prophet but I can hear God. I try not to let people know that I am a minister, but somehow, it always comes up and out. On this line, I have led Praise & Worship, led prayer, preached, led prayer for salvation, and did the Communion.

With my other group, which is a prayer group, I have taught many lessons. In fact, they gave me Worship Wednesday because worship is an essential component of a born-again believer's lifestyle. I want to make sure they understand worship is not just singing. Are you watching me?

While doing ministry, God had another assignment. I was going to Bible Study, and the Lord said, "Turn the car around and go to your sister's." Tell me why we want to argue with God. Don't you remember me saying I can hear God? I told God, "But I have to go to Bible Study." God repeated Himself. I always say when God repeats Himself, He really means business.

So, I went to my sister's. She was so sick. I did everything I could for her that day. She refused to go to the hospital. But I told her I would be back the next day, and if she wasn't doing any better, she was going to the hospital. When I returned the next day, she was worse. I couldn't get her in the car. I had to call "911." They took her to the hospital, and she ended up staying a few days, and I was there every day… all day. Ministry! Watch me!

The Lord has sent me over to my sister's house several times. Sometimes, it's to pray. Sometimes, it's to give Communion.

Sometimes, it is just to sit there and allow her to talk. God help us to be more sensitive to your people.

God allowed me to work for a company for a few months. I thought it was for the money. Sorry! It was strictly "ministry." Even though that company still owes me money, I had a chance to teach some young people how to be professional in a non-professional environment. How to be the best they can be even though the world does not expect it from them because they are young and Black. There is a standard that we all should have in this world. I showed them you can be a born-again believer and stand out in the crowd. I was often told I was different. Yes! Watch me!

Let's take it back a little bit. Right before COVID, I took a position first to assist preschoolers, and then I became an administrator in the front office. Not only was I there to show professionalism, but it became a ministry. First, to the children - they just wanted someone to care. Then it was for the teachers - they needed someone to talk to. Then, to the parents - they needed to know that our positions were not just for a paycheck. We were concerned about the children's education, as well as their welfare. I did some pre-marital counseling. I prayed with people in all types of situations. I prayed for sick children. I jumped in the middle of adults fighting. You name it, I did it!

One morning, I woke up very sick but went to work anyway. When it got unbearable, I drove myself to the emergency room. I was told my blood sugar was 682, stroke level. They said I had diabetes. I said NO, no one in my family had it. I knew this was sent from the devil. Oh yes! He thought he had me. But Jesus honored my prayer. I stayed in the hospital for a week, where they taught me how to use the needle to give myself insulin. I said to the doctors, "Just give me 30 days." I changed my eating habits, lost a little weight, and NO MORE DIABETES! Watch me! I thought about the song, "I'm running for my life, if anybody asks you what's the matter with me, just tell them I'm saved, sanctified, Holy Ghost filled, fire-baptized, I've got Jesus on my side, and I'm running for my life."

When covid came, school was different. They worked from home, and so did I. Everything was challenging. Again, I had to rely on the Holy Spirit both naturally and spiritually. This had NEVER happened. All of the school's calls were transferred to me. Some were nice. Others were not so nice. We had to conduct meetings on Zoom with faculty and parents. Sometimes, I wasn't too happy about doing that. I was cursed out continually. I learned to be patient and keep my mouth closed. I felt like my hands were tied, but I got through it. Again, watch me!

In closing, let me boast on my Lord. I do not look like what I've been through.

I usually sing a song either before I preach or after. If I would choose a song now, it would be "To God be the Glory, for the things He has done." Then, "I Owe it all to Thee" by Norman Hutchins.

I am so thankful that even when I am alone, I am not alone. Why? Because Jesus is with me. The Word says in Deuteronomy 31: 6 (NIV)

> Be strong and courageous. Do not be afraid or terrified because of them, for the Lord your God goes with you; he will never leave you nor forsake you."

I am not going to lie; I do get lonely, but when I do, someone from somewhere calls to say I was on their mind and they were praying. They even ask if I need anything. This is so powerful. God is so wonderful. I don't see how anyone can live in this world without God. Too much is going on out here. This world needs Jesus. This is why we have The Great Commission in Matthew 28:16-20 (KJV):

> Then the eleven disciples went to Galilee, to the mountain where Jesus had told them to go. When they saw him, they worshiped him; but some doubted. Then Jesus came to them and said, "All authority in heaven and on earth has been given to me. Therefore go and make disciples of all nations, baptizing them in the name of the Father and of the Son and of the Holy Spirit, and teaching them to obey everything I have commanded you. And surely I am with you always, to the very end of the age."

RUTH E. KING

"Where He leads me, I will follow, I will go with Him all the way." This has been the battle cry and life theme for this widow, mother, grandmother, sister, spiritual mother, and mentor to many people young and seasoned in the church—graduate of Ambassador Bible Training School in Southfield, MI., Minister Ruth King, licensed Associate Minister of Triumph Church, was first appointed as the Ministry Leader of Decision Time Counselors (taking in souls for Christ) then appointed as the Administrator of Triumph University. She has worked as a teacher/instructor and presider, and now she works in a non-profit organization as an executive director and is a radio show host. She has also worked in public schools as a secretary and mentor to third and fourth-grade girls.

She has been in church all of her life. Prayer and praise are part of her lifestyle, and her home is affectionately called "Prayer Headquarters." She recognizes that one of the greatest weapons against the devil is

PRAYER & PRAISE, praising God in the midst of adversity and pain, knowing that God will give the Victory. She always says, "Praise God, I don't look like what I've been through." Called also an intercessor, she doesn't get much sleep and runs with the mantel of her mother, who was also a great woman of faith. Min. Ruth recognizes that she's called to the nations, and it's time to cry aloud and spare not!

Many doors have opened for her. She served as Choir Director for many years and has had the opportunity to teach and direct alongside some of Detroit's elite musicians. Her transparency during worship compels others to enter God's presence with humility and boldness. She's standing on the Word, knowing she will do "greater works," as the Word of God states. You will find that many people just walk up to her and start talking about their lives. She uses this as a tool to reach the lost and encourage those who feel alone. Min. Ruth is about the Father's Business, and she knows that her steps are ordered by the Lord.

She counts it an honor and privilege to minister to God's people, whether in song, an encouraging word, preaching and/or teaching the Word of God, or prayer. She boldly proclaims, "People, it's not enough to be talented; we need to be anointed! It's the anointing that destroys the yoke."

She does not want to be labeled as a "widow," just called her "Blessed!"

Discovering My Purpose: The Redefinition of Winning
Sheilisa McNeal

Throughout my life's journey, I've grappled with the concepts of success, failure, happiness, loss, and victory. As a self-proclaimed underdog in some aspects of my life, I've come to realize that no matter how much I've accomplished, learned, seen, or done, there are immutable facts about my identity and place in this world that I cannot change. I am a Black woman. Sometimes this is a blessing, other times a curse - situation depending.

I've endured some of the most harrowing traumas and tragedies a human can experience. I was ostracized for my chocolate brown skin tone from as early as I can remember, especially by family members. It wasn't a good look to be the "dark-skinned" child in a family of caramel and fair-skinned folks, but instead of allowing it to completely break my developing self-esteem, I leaned into the mantra of the time and proclaimed that "Black is Beautiful!!" That may sound like a triumph of sorts, but it was more of a coping mechanism than a superpower.

I was also in a physically violent relationship as a teen with the father of my children. For more than three years, I suffered many black eyes and locked jaws, but the hematomas and broken eye sockets paled in comparison to the beatdowns my self-worth took for decades that made me question if I was good enough for anything or anyone.

I've also been blessed with moments of pure joy and profound peace, such as when I walked away from this relationship because God said He did not create me for this purpose. People would later ask how I did it, how did I get the strength to leave? The truth is, one day after packing up once again with my three-year-old and toddler to live in my family's overcrowded apartment, I prayed for God to give me the strength to leave and stay gone. I had to be that specific because I returned numerous times based on promises of better times. But those reunited honeymoon periods didn't last long, and genetics had already compromised my eyesight. So, I had to leave and never return.

After being sexually assaulted and threatened with violence one last time, I knew it would be the last. Because if God gave me the strength, I would never let anyone treat me that way again. He answered that prayer, and no one put their hands on me violently ever again.

These contrasts have taught me the true meaning of relativity. I understand genuine happiness because I've tasted the bitterness of true sadness. I appreciate the power and satisfaction of triumph because I've felt the crushing weight of despair.

Then, there were times when success lifted me so high I believed I could touch the clouds. For example, when I got my first managerial position in corporate right out of college. I made almost $50,000 a year! Something no one in my family had ever done. But I've also known what it's like to be on my knees in my prayer closet, desperately begging God for a breakthrough, feeling I couldn't sink any lower and fearing I wouldn't survive without divine intervention.

One of those times came when the real estate market crashed in 2008, and I lost my primary source of income for an entire year; having left corporate behind more than a decade prior, I was essentially an entrepreneur who did well for several years before the entire market crashed. I reached the point where I was barely scraping by once my savings were exhausted. Eventually, my house went into foreclosure, and for six long years, I was in a constant state of instability and fear.

Through these experiences, I've learned a fundamental truth: loss, pain, and trials are not respecters of persons because my story wasn't mine alone. There were times when I decided I deserved happiness and love but made selfish choices, prioritizing my desires and goals without considering the consequences. In its infinite wisdom, the universe didn't spare me from the fallout of my actions, regardless of my ignorance of potential outcomes.

My faux pas? As a young woman in my early 30s, I became entangled in a torrid soul tie with a man who wasn't honest about his status. A decision that would haunt me for years to come. No, I didn't physically harm anyone, steal, or outright lie to others. But he lied to me, and I lied to myself after I eventually learned the truth. In the process, my lack of self-love and self-worth unjustifiably stole precious time from someone who could never be restored and temporarily compromised my moral and spiritual integrity.

As I said, this indiscretion didn't start that way. This man wove an intricate web of lies, crafting a believable façade about his marital status, his living arrangements, and everything in between. To prove he was indeed single, he invited me to his apartment, and when I noticed a woman's purse, he said it belonged to his ex, who hadn't picked up all her things yet. Then, he spent almost every waking moment with me when he wasn't working or in school. He would pick me up from work in New York City, drive me home to New Jersey, stay the night, and go home around four or five in the morning to shower and get to work by seven. This routine happened regularly, so surely he was single, right? WRONG! And when I finally discovered the truth that the girlfriend was not an ex, who eventually became his wife, I couldn't walk away. I didn't immediately end it.

I justified my actions with the misguided belief that he was in love with me based on his actions, and I reciprocated those feelings. His love, however, was nothing like the selfless, patient, and kind love described in 1 Corinthians 13. I knew better, but I didn't do better until the suffering became unbearable. It took over six years of trying to finally extricate myself from that situation, during which time I hurt someone who had done me no wrong. I never confronted his significant other or made my presence known. Instead, I quietly accepted my role as "second" but decided I was really "first" because that's who he said I was - clinging to the hope that one day, everything would change in my favor, and I'd eventually be his one and only.

But karma, like her evil sister payback, is relentless. I suffered for my actions and weakness. This experience taught me the great lesson of relativity: what goes around comes back. To break the cycle of hurt, you must first change your mind - only then will your behavior follow.

One of my greatest victories was learning to forgive myself for my transgressions after carrying the burden of guilt for more than a decade after it ended. I had spent countless days in prayer and shed innumerable tears in genuine repentance. And, despite knowing that God had answered my prayers for forgiveness, I still felt I deserved to pay a self-imposed penance. But when I finally learned to forgive myself, the weight lifted from my shoulders, and I felt lighter both emotionally and physically. I was no longer carrying guilt like a badge of shame to prove my willingness to accept the consequences of my actions. I was free, and reaching this place was one of my most significant and challenging wins.

Another profound lesson came through parenthood. I realized that no matter how much time, energy, unconditional love, sacrifice, and patience I invested into being a parent, despite having no help from the other biological parent, it wouldn't automatically result in reciprocity from my children. There has been much strife, hurt feelings, and isolation in my relationship with at least one, but sometimes both of my kids. But the win in this situation was in understanding that even if my children never appreciated any of my efforts, it doesn't diminish my value or that I gave them the best life I could. They were never hungry, homeless, or living in squalor. I completed college, even though I was a full-time student, employee, and mom while attending. They were loved by me and their families on both the maternal and paternal sides (despite the absence of their father). I did the best I could.

The truth is, for some children, nothing you do will ever be enough. Your humanity and the inevitable mistakes that stem from ignorance are neither forgiven nor forgotten by your offspring, who expect you to be superhuman despite sharing the same flesh and blood they have.

In the grand scheme of life, I am merely a lumen above dim some days, but that's okay. I'm still learning, still growing, and shining brighter every day that I accept me as I am. I am no longer enslaved by guilt over what I didn't do or didn't know as a teen mom, single parent, or flawed human. I have shed the shackles of past mistakes and bad decisions, having learned from them and gained wisdom in the process.

My children have known me their whole lives, but they don't know about my life before them. They don't truly know who I am at my core. They know the person they've met, what they don't like about their childhood, my shortcomings, and setbacks within their limited frame of reference. And that's okay - life will teach them hard lessons, too, probably in the form of their own sons and daughters. Then, they might change their minds about the ebbs and flows of parenthood, as I did for my mother when I understood I had judged her harshly, and she, too, did her best with what she had.

My win here is that nothing separates my heart from them. I have remained devoted to my children (and their children), even when my heart was broken. I would gladly give my life for theirs because I have been here longer and experienced more. My victory lies in looking at the beautiful individuals they've become with pride, knowing I played a role in shaping them, even if it's never acknowledged. I am grateful for the ability to give life and honor God with my commitment to care for the gifts He's given me. I am even more grateful to understand what it must be like to be God the Father to incorrigible, selfish, judgmental, needy, greedy kids and to love them anyway with an unrelenting, unconditional passion.

My journey of self-discovery and acceptance has been long and arduous, but it's led me to a profound realization: winning is defined by the player in the game. It's not always about the triumphant, fist-pumping moment of glory we see in movies at the end of a race or some other underdog scenario. Sometimes, winning is simply finding and accepting yourself, your voice, and your worth.

I've won because, even after thousands of consecutive days of despair, I never forgot the God who promised never to leave or forsake me. He proved His faithfulness, even when I couldn't see or feel it. My home was in active foreclosure for six years, yet I never lost it because He said, "I won't let them take what I gave you!" Then he literally sent an angel with my mother's name to help me get a permanent modification that had been denied for years by my mortgage company.

I didn't work consistently in any significant capacity for five years, surviving on opportunities that were just enough to get by. Sometimes, I barely scraped by even after working four or five part-time jobs simultaneously. Yet, He sustained me. I lost nothing during this dark time, not even weight (much to my chagrin!). Without health insurance and plagued by numerous health issues, He healed me.

I then thought I found a love that was just for me and married a man with a big heart who turned out to be "monogamy-challenged," but I didn't fall apart. I stayed faithful to my vows and honored the covenant, reaping the reward of repentance. I won when I realized I didn't have to accept his infidelity as penance for my past mistakes. I triumphed when I recognized I was strong enough to walk away without viewing the end of this relationship as a personal failure. One of the hardest lessons of my life!

For a while, I had stopped believing in my dreams. In my lowest and darkest hours, I thought being here was optional. I wasn't suicidal but was totally okay with breathing my last if my time was up. I fantasized someone would find my notes, piece them together, and do my work for me of telling my story as I lay at rest, having exhausted all my energy to fight. But the God I serve wouldn't let that curse come to pass. As my dreams began to retake shape and the possibility of not only penning my story but engaging in even greater acts of humanity unfolded, I began to understand the true definition of faith.

In the Bible, faith is defined as the substance of things hoped for and the evidence of things not seen. For most of my life, I had focused on hope, constantly hoping for something and believing that God, through Christ Jesus, would bring my hopes to fruition. But now I understand that the emphasis should be on substance. Hope implies I'm still waiting for something to happen, but substance is tangible and something I can hold on to, which means I already have it.

Now, I have a different outlook. The things I hope for already exist because there is nothing new under the sun, so it's just a matter of time before it manifests in my life. Faith is about substance, defined as the physical matter of which a person or thing consists of and which has a tangible, solid presence. I just have to remember to place my hope in the Substance of Him, who is Real and Tangible, even though He is Unseen! This revelation marks another win in my column because I finally understand what it means.

I've always been a believer in signs and symbols. The cross holds great symbolic significance for me, and I've come to realize that life is filled with signs and symbols. The substance and evidence of my winning are often symbolized by the most mundane acts.

During my journey of personal rediscovery, all I wanted was to prove to myself that I was who I believed myself to be after losing faith and belief in myself for so long. It seemed that every time I thought a breakthrough had finally come, something happened to let me know, "No... It's not your time yet!" That something was my unbelief! And I would fall deeper into despair.

Day after day, people would tell me how smart, attractive, and accomplished I am. Friends assured me I would get back on my feet, but it felt as if I lived on wet black ice winter, spring, summer, and fall!! Somewhere deep down, I knew there was a winner in me, even when my circumstances contradicted that thought.

Still, my soul never let me completely give up on myself. I stayed true to the Word and became an encourager and advocate for others whose energy resonated with mine. I also became a cheerful giver, even when it meant I would be in lack. I freely gave my time, talents, love, and gifts to those who needed it, no matter what. Even in the face of adversity, this unwavering faith and generosity became a testament to my resilience and character. It's easy to be kind and giving when life is going well, but maintaining that spirit during hardship reveals another layer of character that is often hard to access.

As I reflect on my journey, I'm struck by the profound impact of relativity on our perceptions and experiences. Just as we understand light through darkness and warmth through cold, we truly appreciate joy through sorrow and success through failure. This understanding has transformed my perspective on life's challenges, allowing me to see them not as insurmountable obstacles but as opportunities for growth and self-discovery.

My experiences have taught me that winning isn't always about grand, visible achievements. Sometimes, it's about the quiet victories we achieve within ourselves - overcoming fear, forgiving ourselves and others, or simply getting up each day to face the world with renewed hope and determination when all you want to do is lay in the dark and disappear.

I have learned that true strength lies in vulnerability. By acknowledging my weaknesses and mistakes, I have found a power I never knew I possessed. My honesty with myself has allowed me to forge deeper, more authentic connections with others and approach life with a newfound sense of purpose and clarity. This journey of self-acceptance has been perhaps my greatest challenge and my most significant victory.

For years, I struggled with the gap between who I thought I should be and who I am. I chased an idealized version of myself, constantly feeling like I fell short. But through my trials and tribulations, I've come to embrace my imperfections, recognizing that they are an integral part of who I am.

My journey has also taught me the importance of gratitude. Even in my darkest moments, when everything seemed to fall apart, I found small things to be thankful for. I now write in my gratitude journal almost daily. This practice has become a lifeline, helping me maintain perspective and find hope on the inevitable good and bad days.

I now approach each day with a sense of curiosity and wonder, eager to learn and grow. I've let go of the need for perfection and instead embraced progress. I celebrate small victories. I've found joy in the journey itself rather than fixating solely on the end goal. This shift in perspective has transformed not only how I view myself but also how I interact with the world around me.

I'm more compassionate towards others, understanding that everyone is fighting their own battles. I'm quicker to offer help and slower to judge. I've learned the power of kindness and how a small act of generosity can have a ripple effect, touching lives in ways we may never fully comprehend.

Ultimately, I have realized that the true measure of winning isn't found in external validation or material success. It is found in the person we become through our struggles and triumphs. It's in the lives we touch, the love we share, and the legacy we leave behind.

By this measure, I can confidently say that I am winning - not because my life is perfect or because I have achieved all my goals, but because I continue to believe anything is possible. My story is far from over. In fact, I know for sure the best is yet to come. After all, I was created by Greatness to be and do Great Things!

SHEILISA MCNEAL

Sheilisa McNeal is a passionate writer, entrepreneur, mother, and grandmother who advocates for personal growth, resilience, and self-love. With a life story marked by profound challenges, including trauma, heartbreak, and the complexities of parenthood, Sheilisa has emerged as a voice of hope and inspiration. Her journey from feeling like an underdog to embracing her true self has fueled her desire to help others navigate their own struggles. In addition to her writing, Sheilisa is the founder and CEO of Fria Inc., a fem-tech startup that creates innovative wearable cooling accessories designed to alleviate the discomfort of hot flashes and overheating. Through her writing and entrepreneurial ventures, she shares lessons from her experiences, emphasizing the importance of forgiveness, faith, and the power of the relentless spirit. Sheilisa believes that winning is defined by the individual and that true success lies in personal growth and the connections we foster with others.

MY DELICACY OF SOCIETY
JUNE SMITH

I Am Me!

I am the beauty of mountains laden with colorful, vibrant flowers.

I am my inner voice, no longer silent.

I am the utopic essence of life.

I am nature's rain falling on me.

I am the fabric of "unlimitedness."

I am mine to explore, I have become unstoppable!

Copyright 2010 JSB

PREFACE: THE STORIES WE LEAVE BEHIND AND THE LIVES WE TOUCH

This story is designed to help you witness the similarities of the circle of interaction between the building process of an initiative and that of its creator.

We go through the day hoping that our expectations will be met, our feelings will be respected, and, in turn, everything will go our way. We are often taught to visualize positive things, which will materialize into all we hope for. Somehow, no matter how mature we become, no one prepares us for when we are ambushed by real-life occurrences. Experiences considered life-altering, life-shattering, and life-changing shake our very foundations and rock us to the core in ways that we cannot articulate or recover from as quickly as we had hoped.

The term "Delicacies of Society" refers to the very thing creatives are. They are delicate pearls of wisdom and exquisite talent who are, at times, fragile beings who may have encountered trauma or pain yet have resiliently risen to produce strength, beauty, and perseverance as their superpower.

According to the Center for Disease Control (CDC)[1] adolescents aged 12-17 years in 2018-2019 reported 15.1% had a major depressive episode, 36.7% had persistent feelings of sadness or hopelessness, 4.1% had a substance use disorder, 1.6% had an alcohol use disorder, 3.2% had an illicit drug use disorder, 18.8% seriously considered attempting suicide, 15.7% made a suicide plan, 8.9% attempted suicide, and 2.5% made a suicide attempt requiring medical treatment.

Recently, I traveled to Thailand to explore more of myself and better define my purpose. I bought a funky travel journal to help capture some of my life-changing moments. Over two weeks and a 19-hour flight each way, I captured a few pages of thoughts but returned home with loads

---

[1] https://www.cdc.gov/childrensmentalhealth/data.html

of pictures, great memories, and feeling full yet empty simultaneously. Fast forward, as I approached the end months of the year, I came close to losing my life; I was experiencing changes in my business and watching my family dynamics shift. I suddenly felt trapped with a multitude of emotions.

I found myself questioning my purpose and searching to find my place in this new phase of life. Throughout my life, I have experienced tough and challenging times; I've been homeless and have been in relationships with great men, loving men, sexy men, beautiful men, fake men, and selfish men. However, I never experienced men who valued me for me, for my heart, for my support, for my authenticity, or for my mind. I recently discovered an anonymous quote in the MindsJournal that said, "You're rare, so people are gonna fall in love with the idea of having you, but most of them aren't used to rare; they're foreign to it, so they'll lack the capacity to treat you as such. And that's where they lose you." Hmmmm, that very profound quote resonated instantly with me.

Why am I sharing this? Who really cares? I am sharing this because I believe that throughout my relationships, platonic or romantic, I never valued myself enough to notice that my depression was the impetus for the inability to dig deep and lean into me. It was easier to pour into others. It was debilitating to scrape every layer of flesh and inspect it with care to see that my creation was not in vain. I needed to see and believe that the self-portrait of me was not indicative of how others saw me and validated me or not. The rabbit hole we fall into is often built upon other people's opinions. It allows us to see and adopt false narratives. The false narrative propels poor decisions, which allows for the flow, and we end up in the stream of resistance called anxiety and stress.

Nothing good ever comes from resisting the flow of energy. I have lived it, seen it, and received two hoodies, a T-shirt, and a hat for it. I am exiting stage left. If you know anything about the arts, you know that coming off stage allows you to prepare for the next scene. It also allows you to reassess your performance and regroup. While preparing for the next scene/spotlight, if there is another opportunity for the spotlight, you are breathing and exhaling.

I am this initiative Art In June. My wonderfully brilliant daughters reminded me of the nuggets of wisdom I implanted into them that are now necessary to water my own garden of transformation. We sometimes forget that to be good teachers and parents, we must be good students and learners. We must be comfortable with eating our own words and being vulnerable. We must be comfortable with letting the words permeate our spirits to help us unbecome so that we can Be. Often, "Being" is the thing that we ask God for. It is the guidance that, when placed in front of us, we miss the subtle signs because we are busy searching for what we think we need to Be.

My gift is writing. It is how I have made a living for many years, what I studied in college, my favorite pastime as a child, and it is in my DNA.

It is my pain and my pleasure. Although I often run from it, I find myself coming back to it. It is like a jilted lover who causes me pain, but somehow, I can't resist the passion of our toxic union.

Art In June: Delicacies of Society is the initiative I founded to explore art and mental health. On a larger scale, it is an opportunity to raise awareness as we unveil stories of creatives like me who have their own struggles in the midst of their creative process yet find a way to produce the most inspiring and captivating artwork, performances, literature, etc. Despite their challenges, I will simply be grateful if Art In June: Delicacies Of Society allows you to take the pearl within and offer it to the world as your diamond of greatness. I will be grateful if you can have a new perspective on how you see yourself, how you see Art and the arts, and how you prioritize placement for your mental wellness in today's society.

"Your greatest growth comes from your lowest times."- MEejie

PART I: THE MIGRATION

My mother was a single parent who always worked at least two jobs six days a week, sang opera, and listened to classical music in her spare time. My father, a Pastor, was in my orbit until the age of 5 and left only to resurface intermittently in my adult life. My birth certificate never bore his name, but I always knew his name, and I would occasionally spend time at his family's home in the country. As a child, he was never there; therefore, I could recall very little about our interactions. Our final moments of communication were closer to his final days of life.

I knew I had sisters but had no way of finding them. God would align things in such a way that four months after my mother's death, through the funeral home's death announcement and obituary, my sisters (who resembled me and my father) would find me.

I grew up accustomed to the life that my mother provided. My life started in Trinidad, West Indies. At age 10, I migrated to America for what I thought was a holiday vacation to visit my mother, who had migrated four to five years prior. Instead, it was my mother's creative way of permanently relocating my sister and me for a new life and a better foundation in the land paved with streets of gold.

I never returned to my school, St Hilda's, ever again, but found myself navigating the nuisances of two worlds. Encapsulated in a culture shock of sorts, my familiarity was gone, my friends were gone, my confidence diminished, but my curiosity expanded and made me inquisitive. The food was different. The air smelled like the boxes of clothing my mother would send home from the USA. The weather was unlike anything I could have imagined, and the people's accents seemed very sophisticated, while mine was described as rhythmic. I often felt like a square peg in a round hole. I watched a lot of television; some shows were familiar, and others were unfamiliar but enveloping. I thought school was intriguing and frustrating, and although the culture was foreign, I managed.

As I progressed as a teenager, I made a few friends along the way, matriculated through high school, and was college-bound. I studied Journalism and Mass Communications and English at Rutgers University. As many classmates and associates often interrogated me about my culture, I became a sponge that soaked up characteristics, personalities, and idiosyncrasies. I created movies in my head, and media and the arts became a way of life. I enjoyed exploring the underside of things. Imagination, innovation, and introspection became my whys. I wanted to learn how to apply my skills and knowledge to improve my life and my family. Although I was the youngest daughter of my mother, I recall how much she sacrificed. I wanted to make sure that I helped her by helping myself. It would be the strategy that shaped my perspective on life and living.

PART II: A DISCOVERY

In addition to finding my father for the second time and meeting and learning about my new four sisters, I would experience the loss of seven relatives of differing ages within three years. I capped off 2023 fighting for my life and becoming hospitalized for a week with influenza and pneumonia.

As I struggled to recover in the hospital in isolation, I was not only extremely sick, but I experienced substandard care from the hospital staff. I believe physicians and other medical personnel are true, authentic warriors. My concern becomes tunnel-focused, however, based on the disparity issues that Black and Brown people in this country often experience. My hospital room had beautiful beige walls with one painting that lacked interest and hence did nothing for my palliative care and/or mental health. I started wondering about individuals experiencing mental health episodes or senior citizens who are without advocates. What does their overall health and/or mental health journey become? As a creative, I began pondering the connection between art and palliative care. Is there a way to amplify and expand mental health awareness? If so, is there a way to learn more about mental health challenges during the creative process? I was forced to rethink what strategy could be implemented to shape the correlation between mental health and art. What do I need to know or learn about creatives and their challenges as they enter their creative process? As I prepared to launch this initiative, I realized that all of the steps and research needed to execute this initiative had to start with me. My present life was the mirror to the layers of the creative inner soul journey that I was exploring in others. I was forced to examine my insecurities, challenges, concerns, and mental health. Our mental wellness is based on our mind, body, and spirit becoming aligned.

Alignment, by definition, is simply an adjustment to a line. The search for my alignment required me to examine the connection between my work, thoughts, and childhood experiences to my purpose. As I talk about my childhood experiences, I recall a story about my childhood friend Zoya, a 9-year-old inquisitive analytical thinker. She, too, like me, had siblings, and we lived in a community with musicians, artists, housekeepers, and blue-collared, hard-working folks who believed in keeping their property clean, but they also had stories and secrets tucked away in the closets of their souls. They praised God in the Anglican churches but would attend the Catholic church for prayer and absolution of their sins.

Moreover, many would pass by the Shango center and witness worshippers dressed in white catching the Holy Ghost. I recall my mother warning me not to go near them or interact with them. Zoya, on the other hand, was curious. She wanted to know and understand why, what, who, and where. She wanted to understand the difference between the Catholic school we attended and the festivities of the Shango people we would hear worshipping as we went back and forth from school. When it's said and done, isn't that why we were enrolled in school? Isn't that the reason we read books and listened to lectures?

As kids, we explored; we were nosey and laughed at everything except the one rainy Sunday afternoon when Zoya perched herself by her window to watch the rain fall on the concrete streets, only to witness our neighbor Ms. Sheena running down the street naked, with a full face of makeup. Ms. Sheena was a neighbor who lived with her sister and older brothers in a big, regal house with white railings. Ms. Sheena was a nice lady who worked in a nearby factory. She was always well-dressed, pleasant and friendly. This Sunday afternoon was an exception. Something happened. Zoya was in disbelief as she recalled her mother running out of their house with a robe to cover Ms. Sheena.

The ambulance came and took her away, and we never saw her again. Zoya recalled how that one incident shook her up, so much so that she never forgot it, but she couldn't comprehend it either. I likened her experience to another Sunday afternoon when I witnessed a man brutally beating a scantily clad woman in front of our house. If you know anything about Caribbean neighborhoods, sometimes small canals empty into bigger rivers (those canals can sometimes run right through the neighborhoods). As this woman tried to escape a relentless flogging, she slipped and fell into the moss-filled canal, screaming for help! The men gambling on the block jumped in to help her as she came out crying, soaked, and embarrassed. I remember wondering, how could someone do that? What did this lady do to warrant a public beating? I, too, could not understand, but it stained my brain. A few months later, I was on a plane to America and never had a chance to talk to Zoya. I often wondered how she felt about that Sunday afternoon and if it was similar to my feelings and emotions. Reflecting as an adult, we were witnesses of trauma, domestic violence, and mental health challenges that possibly yielded from pain, sorrow, anger, and anguish. There was no way for my young mind to subconsciously reconcile how those experiences affected me except to suggest that they carved a pathway to bad relationships, domestic abuse, and the sexual molestation that I encountered.

My delicacy duty is waking up and realizing that despite the really painful, humiliating times in my life, I look nothing like my trauma and pain. Despite a job loss, deficiencies in my bank account, bouts of depression, and health challenges, my faith in God never wavered. I am sometimes angry and disappointed with God. I often share with God my disappointment with His universal snail's pace of activity. Somehow, I still celebrate victorious endings to life's drama. Synergy and alignment, though positive concepts to embrace, can also sometimes appear "wonky." However, even at my lowest points, I always found reasons that invigorated my zest for living. Growing up in poverty can greatly affect one's mental wellness. It can also generate so much despair that suicide attempts become possible options. I understand, I empathize, and I grieve for those who couldn't find a way to make the pain disappear.

As serendipitous as my challenges mentally and figuratively have been in pushing this Art In June: Delicacies of Society initiative forward, I am bringing the Zoyas and Ms. Sheenas, and the ladies who fall in canals, and the hard-working men and women in my Trinidadian and American villages to the forefront. I am excited about bringing them all with me to share in the liberation from mental slavery because God has allowed me additional time on the playground. I am amplifying that mental wellness is paramount to surviving in this world. I am happy to be the guinea piglet to testify that art is vital to my sustainability (and perhaps all of our sustainability) because it is another source of oxygen. Art has become my superpower. As I connect my writing and artistry with my spiritual "groundedness," I realize that meditation, the sound bowl, sage, exercise, music, prayers, and solitude provide a toolkit of armor and survival for the wars ahead.

Booker T. Washington poignantly taught me to remember, "Success is to be measured not so much by the position that one has reached in life as by the obstacles which he has overcome while trying to succeed." I hope readers glean that passion and purpose are what truly make the art in this June a true delicacy of society. The interconnectedness one experiences between art therapy and mental health has several benefits that should not be ignored. It is my hope that after reading my story, you will consider sharing it with others; more importantly, you will engage in some form of art that will allow you to begin to experience the possibilities of stress reduction, better physical health, improvement in your cognitive abilities and your self-esteem. Who knows, you may find that you, too, may be chosen for a new purpose.

JUNE SMITH

June Smith is an art lover, art collector, and an entrepreneur at heart. Born in Trinidad, West Indies, she migrated to the United States at age ten and was raised in the arts. June has a dynamically varied background in publishing, business, education, and entertainment. A published writer and graduate of Rutgers University, June has worked with a multitude of brilliant professionals at PricewaterhouseCoopers, Simon and Schuster, the New York Department of Education, and Noelle Elaine Media, among others. She is the founder of Art In June: Delicacies Of Society, an initiative designed to examine the correlation between art and mental health. An advocate for holistic living, June has been very transparent about her experience with depression. June believes that proper mental wellness is extremely vital. June resides in the New York metro area and is passionate about raising awareness around mental health. In her free time, June enjoys writing, music, and creating.

9 780999 855166